P9-ARK-324

TELL ME WHY, TELL ME HOW

HOW DO BEES MAKE HONEY?

MELISSA STEWART

Marshall Cavendish
Benchmark
New York

Marshall Cavendish Benchmark
99 White Plains Road
Tarrytown, NY 10591-5502
www.marshallcavendish.us

All Web sites were available and accurate when this book was sent to press.

Library of Congress Cataloging-in-Publication Data
Stewart, Melissa.
How do bees make honey? / by Melissa Stewart.
p. cm. — (Tell me why, tell me how)
Summary: "Provides comprehensive information on bees and the process of how they make honey"—Provided by publisher.
Includes index.
ISBN 978-0-7614-2923-4
1. Honey—Juvenile literature. 2. Honeybees—Juvenile literature. I. Title. II. Series.

SF539.S74 2009
638'.16—dc22

2007022935

Photo research by Candlepants Incorporated.

Cover Photo: SuperStock Inc. / Super Stock

The photographs in this book are used by permission and through the courtesy of:
Minden Pictures: Konrad Wothe, 1; Michael Durham, 5, 22; Stephen Dalton, 14, 23; Kim Taylor/Npl, 15, 18, 19.
Super Stock: Age Fotostock, 4, 13; Mauritius, 6. *Photo Researchers Inc.*: Dr. Jeremy Burgess, 8; W. Treat Davidson, 10; Sinclair Stammers, 17. *Corbis*: Herbert Zetti, 9; Craig Tuttle, 21; Martin Jepp/Zefa, 24; Bichon/Photocuisine, 25.
Animals Animals-Earth Scenes: Donald Specker, 12, 20; Maria Zorn, 16.

Editor: Joy Bean
Publisher: Michelle Bisson
Art Director: Anahid Hamparian
Series Designer: Alex Ferrari

Printed in Malaysia
1 3 5 6 4 2

CONTENTS

This honeybee spends its days traveling from flower to flower. It is collecting nectar to make honey.

The Buzz on Honeybees

At least twenty thousand different kinds, or **species,** of bees live on Earth today. But only seven of these species can make honey. They are called honeybees.

When a honeybee spots a brightly colored flower, it comes in for a landing.

The first bees probably lived in Africa about one hundred million years ago. Today, they can be found on every continent except one. There are no bees on Antarctica.

Ancient cave paintings in Europe and Africa show that people have been collecting honey from wild bee nests, or **hives,** for at least ten thousand years. People started keeping honeybees in human-made hives about five thousand years ago.

Today, most of our food is sweetened with sugar or corn syrup.

This jar of honey was made from nectar that bees collected from millions of flowers.

But until about 250 years ago, most people relied on honey to make sweet treats. They did not know how to remove sugar from sugarcane or how to make corn syrup from corn. Today, the average American eats a little more than 1 pound (0.5 kilograms) of honey each year.

Now I Know!

How long have people been collecting honey from beehives?

At least ten thousand years.

A bee uses its strawlike proboscis
to suck up flower nectar.

Food from Flowers

During the warm months of the year, thousands of honeybees fly from the hive just after sunrise. Over the next twelve hours, each bee will have visited more than a thousand flowers.

At each stop, a bee uses its long, strawlike **proboscis** to suck up thin, runny **nectar**. The sugary liquid is a good source of energy for the little insects. As it is being collected, some of the nectar travels down a tube to the bee's stomach. But most of it flows down a second tube to the bee's **honey sac**, so it can be taken back to the hive and made into honey.

Each time a honeybee lands on a flower, bits of powdery **pollen** stick to its body. The

As a bee collects nectar, pollen sticks to its body.

9

insect rolls the pollen into balls and carries the balls in tiny pollen baskets on its back legs. The pollen is a good source of protein and vitamins, which bees need to live and grow.

After visiting about one hundred flowers, the bee's weight has nearly doubled. The honey sac contains so much nectar that it has stretched to fill most of the bee's **abdomen**. The little insect makes a beeline back to the hive and quickly

This bee's pollen basket is full. Soon it will fly back to the hive and drop off its load.

unloads its cargo. Then it heads back out to search for more nectar and pollen.

A honeybee usually collects about ten loads of food each day. In North America, honeybees visit clovers, dandelions, berry bushes, and fruit tree blossoms. These plants produce plenty of nectar and pollen to attract bees, butterflies, and other insects.

As a bee flies from one plant to the next, some of the pollen that gets stuck to its body falls off. When a **sperm cell** inside the pollen **fuses** with an **egg cell** inside the flower, a fruit begins to grow. If the seeds inside the fruit land in rich, moist soil, they will develop into new plants. Many plants could not reproduce without the help of bees and other insects.

Honeybees only go out in search of nectar and pollen on warm, sunny days. But they need food to eat all year long. Because nectar is almost 80 percent water, storing enough of the sweet stuff to feed a hive full of honeybees all winter long would take up a great deal of room. To save space, the bees change the nectar into honey— a thick, syrupy liquid that is only about 18 percent water.

Now I Know!

Name two things honeybees collect from flowers.

Nectar and pollen.

11

In the summertime, a hive like this one may house thirty thousand honeybees.

Inside the Hive

Most species of bees live alone. But honeybees live in large groups called **colonies**. Most honeybee colonies include twenty thousand to thirty thousand bees. But some may have as many as one hundred thousand members. That's a lot of bees in one place!

A honeybee colony lives inside a hive. In warm parts of the world, honeybees build hives in sheltered places, such as inside hollow trees or deep rock crevices. Most of the honeybees in the United States and Canada, however, live in human-made hives. They are

The modern movable frame hive was developed in 1852. It allows a beekeeper to inspect the hive and remove honey without harming the colony.

looked after by people called beekeepers.

Inside a hive, rows of honeycombs hang close together. Each honeycomb is made of wax and contains hundreds of small, six-sided cells. Bees store honey in the cells near the top of the hive. Pollen is stored below the honey. The cells at the bottom of the hive are full of young bees.

Every honeybee starts its life as a tiny egg inside a honeycomb cell. After a few days, the egg's outer shell melts away and a wormlike grub appears. The little **larva** barely moves.

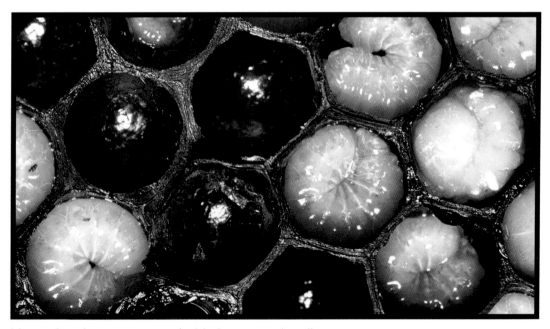

Honey bee larvae grow up inside honeycomb cells.

As adult bees feed it a steady supply of food, the grub grows quickly. Every few days, the larva **molts**, or sheds its skin.

After four to nine days, the grub molts for the last time and spins a cocoon around itself. Now it is a **pupa**. Adult bees cover the opening of the pupa's cell with a thin coat of wax. For the next ten days to three weeks, the developing insect will go through many changes. All of its body parts break down and rearrange themselves. Finally, the new adult chews its way out of its cell.

These pupae are silent and still, but their insides are going through many changes.

15

The queen bee lays eggs all day and all night. She may lay more than one million eggs during her life,

The Honeybees' Roles

Not all of the honeybees in a colony are the same. They are different sizes and they have different roles. Each colony has one queen. She is the most important member. During spring and summer, the queen lays about 1,500 eggs every day. As long as the queen is healthy, she releases a chemical that makes all the other bees in the colony feel safe and calm.

In addition to the queen, a colony has about two hundred drones. These are male bees that live for no more than a few

A drone bee is a bit smaller than a queen. It lives for just a few days to a few weeks.

weeks. They do not have stingers, so they cannot protect themselves from enemies. And drones cannot eat because they do not have mouthparts. Their only job is to mate with queens from other colonies.

Most of the bees in a colony are workers. These female bees are much smaller than the queen and the drones. They spend their days building honeycombs, cleaning cells, collecting food and water, caring for the growing grubs, and guarding the hive.

Young workers are assigned to "house duty." Their job is to stay inside the hive and clean out cells and feed the queen and grubs. These house bees quickly learn that the youngest grubs eat **royal jelly**—a nutritious, milky syrup made inside the bees' bodies. After three days, most of the grubs begin eating **bee bread**—a mixture of honey and pollen. Grubs that will

These busy worker bees are cleaning out cells and making honey.

18

become new queens continue to eat only royal jelly.

When a worker bee is about two weeks old, she becomes a builder. She spends her time adding new cells to the honeycomb structures inside the hive. The bee releases flakes of wax from special **glands** on her abdomen and carefully shapes them into six-sided cells.

About a week later, the worker bee switches jobs again. Now she focuses on changing thin, runny nectar into thick, rich honey.

After about four days, the worker bee becomes a guard. This means that during the day, she patrols the area around the hive. She is on the lookout for bears, badgers, or other animals that might attack the hive and steal the colony's

The underside of the honeybee is seen here, where the abdomenal wax glands (circled above) are located.

See this honeybee's stinger? If the bee uses it to attack an enemy, the bee will die.

honey. If the bee spots an enemy, she signals the other guards and they attack. Honeybees only sting intruders if they have no other choice. When a bee injects an enemy with poison, its stinger is ripped from its body and the little insect dies.

If the bee survives guard duty, she will finally become a field bee and travel out in search of nectar and pollen. Over the next three weeks, the bee will collect food from dawn until dusk.

During all those trips, the bee will collect enough nectar to produce only a tiny amount of honey. But because so many worker bees are helping, some colonies can produce up to 2 pounds (1 kg) of honey a day. To make all that honey, the workers must travel more than 100,000 miles (161,000 kilometers) and suck nectar from about four million flowers.

Most worker bees die after about six weeks, but workers that hatch from their eggs in late summer usually live through the winter. During the cold months, they stay inside the hive and care for the queen. Most queen bees live for as long as four years. During that time, they may lay more than one million eggs.

A field of flowers provides hundreds of bees with the nectar they need to produce honey.

Now I Know!

Name three kinds of honeybees that live in a hive.

Queens, drones, and workers.

21

This bee's pollen basket
looks about half full. It can
visit more flowers before
its basket is completely full.

How Do Bees Make Honey?

When a field bee returns to the hive with a honey sac full of nectar, she forces the nectar back up into her mouth. Then a house bee places the tip of her tubelike tongue on the tip of the field bee's tongue. She sucks the nectar out of the field bee's mouth and into her own honey sac.

A house bee (right) sucks the nectar out of a field bee's (left) honey sac.

These house bees are turning nectar into honey.

Over the next few hours, the house bee begins changing the nectar into honey. She forces small amounts of thin, runny nectar into her mouth and rolls it around. Chemicals in the bee's **saliva**, or spit, break down the sugars in the nectar. This makes the energy-rich food easier to digest. The chemicals also help to keep the sugary liquid fresh for a long time.

The honey in these jars will stay fresh for months due to chemicals in bee's saliva.

After about twenty minutes, the bee spreads the nectar-honey along the tops of the cells in the honeycomb. Then other house bees fan their wings over the cells, causing the water in the nectar-honey to **evaporate**, or change to a gas and rise into the air. After about five days, most of the water is gone. What is left behind? A sugary syrup that is thick and sticky, nutritious, and delicious. It is honey.

Worker bees gather the honey, pour it into a clean cell, and cap it with a thin layer of wax. The honey will be stored here until the bees eat it.

Activity

Most field bees focus on just one kind of flower during each collecting trip. House bees do not mix nectar from different flowers as they make honey. As a result, the color, flavor, and thickness of honey produced depends on the kind of flower the nectar came from.

To see how nectar from various flowers can make different kinds of honey, collect the following materials:

several different kinds of honey
spoons
a pencil and paper

1. Look carefully at each type of honey. Make a chart and write down any differences you notice.
2. Pour a sample of each honey onto a spoon. Are some kinds of honey thicker than others? Write down any differences you notice.

3. Taste a spoonful of each honey. How does each taste? Write down any differences you notice.
4. Have a friend repeat steps one through three. Compare your answers. Does what your friend wrote suprise you?

Glossary

abdomen—The back section of an insect's body.

bee bread—A mixture of honey and pollen. It is fed to developing worker bees and drones beginning at four days old.

colony—A group of bees that lives together.

egg cell—A reproductive cell found inside flowers and female animals.

evaporate—To change from a liquid state to a gas that rises into the air.

fuse—To join together.

gland—A body structure that makes and releases materials an animal needs. Honeybees have glands that produce wax.

hive—The nest or human-made structure in which bees live.

honey sac—A pouch in a bee's abdomen that holds nectar temporarily.

larva (pl. **larvae**)—The second stage in the life of some insects. The term is also used to describe young amphibians and some other kinds of animals.

molt—To shed an old outer covering that has become too small.

nectar—A sugary liquid that many flowers produce. It attracts insects that spread the plant's pollen.

pollen—A sticky powder that must be spread from one flower to another in order for a plant to reproduce.

proboscis—A long, tonguelike structure that bees use to suck up nectar.

pupa (pl. **pupae**)—The third stage in the life of some insects.

royal jelly—A nutritious, milky syrup made inside the bodies of worker bees. All bee grubs eat it for their first three days of life. After that, grubs that will become queens continue to eat royal jelly. Bees that will become workers or drones are switched to bee bread.

saliva—A watery liquid that contains chemicals that aid in the digestion of food.

species—A group of similar creatures that can mate and produce healthy young.

sperm cell—A reproductive cell found in plant pollen and male animals.

Find Out More

BOOKS

Allen, Judy. *Are You a Bee?* Boston: Kingfisher, 2004.

Milton, Joyce. *Honeybees*. New York: Grosset & Dunlap, 2003.

Starosta, Paul. *The Bee: Friend of the Flowers*. Watertown, MA: Charlesbridge, 2005.

WEB SITES

The Buzz About Bees

http://www.pbs.org/wgbh/nova/bees/buzz.html
From PBS's NOVA Web site, information about bees.

Honeybee

http://www.gpnc.org/honeybee.htm
From the Great Plains Nature Center, a look into the lives of bees.

Honey Bees

http://honeybee.tamu.edu/
The official honeybee Web site from Texas A&M University's Department of Entomology.

Index

Page numbers for illustrations are in **boldface.**